BEADING

FOR FUN!

By Benjamin Ashfield

Content Adviser: Tammy Tiranasar, Beading Artist, New York City
Reading Adviser: Frances J. Bonacci, Ed.D, Reading Specialist, Cambridge, Massachusetts

COMPASS POINT BOOKS

MINNEAPOLIS, MINNESOTA

Compass Point Books
3109 West 50th Street, #115
Minneapolis, MN 55410

Visit Compass Point Books on the Internet at www.compasspointbooks.com
or e-mail your request to custserv@compasspointbooks.com

Photographs ©: Photos.com, front cover, 44 (bottom right); Darren Greenwood/Age Fotostock, 4-5; Lowell Georgia/Corbis, 6-7; Shutterstock, 8-9; Scott B. Rosen, 10 (left), 12 (bottom), 13 (left), 15, 21, 22-23, 24, 25, 26, 27, 28, 29, 30–31, 32-33, 38-39; Photodisc/Getty Images, 10-11 (center); Ingram Publishing, 12 (top); Photodisc, 13 (right), 44 (left); Corel, 14, 42 (left), 44 (top), 45 (left), 47; Istockphoto, 16-17, 42 (center and right), 43 (bottom); AP Wide World Photos, 35, 36-37, 37, 39 (right), 41, 43 (top left and top right), 45 (right)

Editors: Deb Berry and Aubrey Whitten/Bill SMITH STUDIO; and Shelly Lyons
Designer/Page Production: Geron Hoy, Kavita Ramchandran, Sinae Sohn, Marina Terletsky, and Brock Waldron/Bill SMITH STUDIO
Photo Researcher: Jacqueline Lissy Brustein, Scott Rosen, and Allison Smith/Bill SMITH STUDIO
Art Director: Jaime Martens
Creative Director: Keith Griffin
Editorial Director: Carol Jones
Managing Editor: Catherine Neitge
Illustrator: Antoine Clarke

Library of Congress Cataloging-in-Publication Data

Ashfield, Benjamin.
  Beading for fun! / by Benjamin Ashfield.
     p. cm. -- (For fun!)
  Includes bibliographical references and index.
  ISBN 0-7565-1688-9 (hard cover)
  1. Beadwork. I. Title. II. Series.
  TT860.A75 2005
  745.58'2--dc22
                                2005030253

Printed in the United States of America.

Table of Contents

The Basics

Doing It

People, Places, and Fun

Note: In this book, there are two kinds of vocabulary words. Beading Words to Know are words specific to beading. They are defined on page 46. Other Words to Know are helpful words that aren't related only to beading. They are defined on page 47.

The Joy of Beading

Have you ever found a colorful pebble on the ground and taken it home with you? Do you like to pick up seashells from the beach? Maybe you have a shoebox full of old buttons in your room at home. With the art of beading, you can use all that you find to make necklaces, bracelets, and more.

Beading is a fun and exciting way to decorate almost anything. You start by collecting beads from materials you see all around you. You can also buy beads in every color, shape, and texture imaginable. When you attach beads together on a string it is called beading.

People throughout history have used beads to decorate their clothes and bodies. Before we start working on our own beading projects, let's look at what some other creative people have done.

How It All Began

Beads have been a part of every culture throughout history. Archaeologists have found beads in Egyptian tombs, Roman catacombs, and Native American burial sites. All kinds of shells, animal claws, seeds, teeth, bones, stones, metals, and glass have been made into beads. Special beads were very valuable. In earlier times, only wealthy families could afford beaded clothing and jewelry.

For ancient cultures, the colors and patterns in beadwork had special meaning. The ancient Egyptians wore beads to bring them luck and to protect them from misfortune. They most valued blue stones, such as lapis lazuli, which they believed would protect good health.

Native Americans made small tubular beads called wampum from clam shells. These beads were used as money by the first Native Americans, who traded with the colonists.

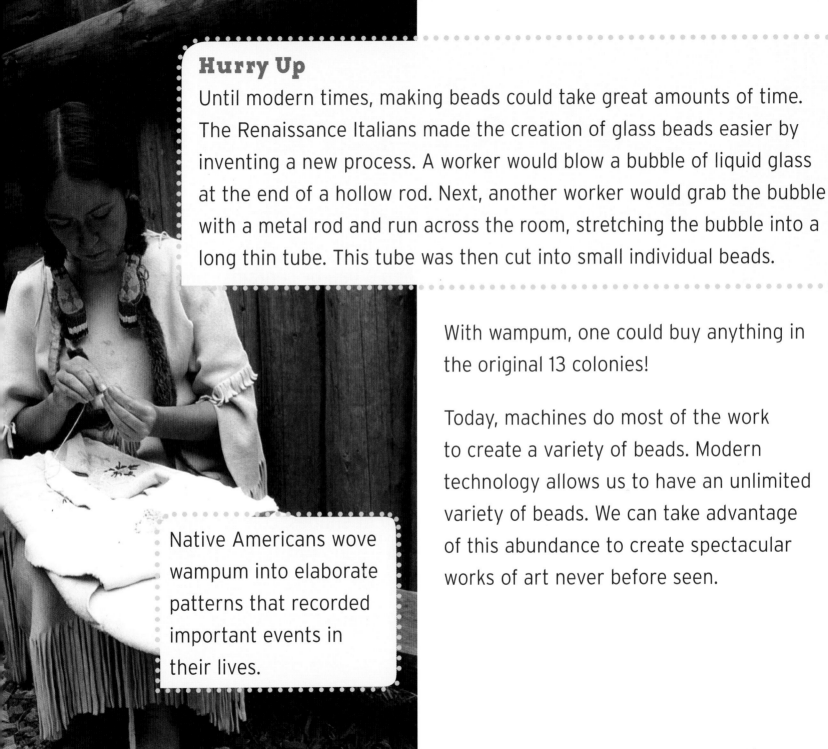

Hurry Up

Until modern times, making beads could take great amounts of time. The Renaissance Italians made the creation of glass beads easier by inventing a new process. A worker would blow a bubble of liquid glass at the end of a hollow rod. Next, another worker would grab the bubble with a metal rod and run across the room, stretching the bubble into a long thin tube. This tube was then cut into small individual beads.

With wampum, one could buy anything in the original 13 colonies!

Today, machines do most of the work to create a variety of beads. Modern technology allows us to have an unlimited variety of beads. We can take advantage of this abundance to create spectacular works of art never before seen.

Native Americans wove wampum into elaborate patterns that recorded important events in their lives.

7

Beads Beyond Belief

Where do beads come from? Nearly everywhere! Beads can be found while you are on a walk in the woods, on the beach, or around your neighborhood. Keep a bag or container handy and be on the lookout for pebbles, seeds, and seashells with a small hole in them. Look around your house, too. Extra buttons make great beads. Garage sales and flea markets sell old jewelry that you can take apart and use in your own projects. Keep your eyes open and soon you will gather a large collection of things to string.

Craft stores carry beads in a variety of shapes, colors, and textures. Of course there are simple round beads, but there are more choices available. There is no limit to the silly, fun, and beautiful shapes you might find. Sparkling beads can add a lot of charm to any beaded creation.

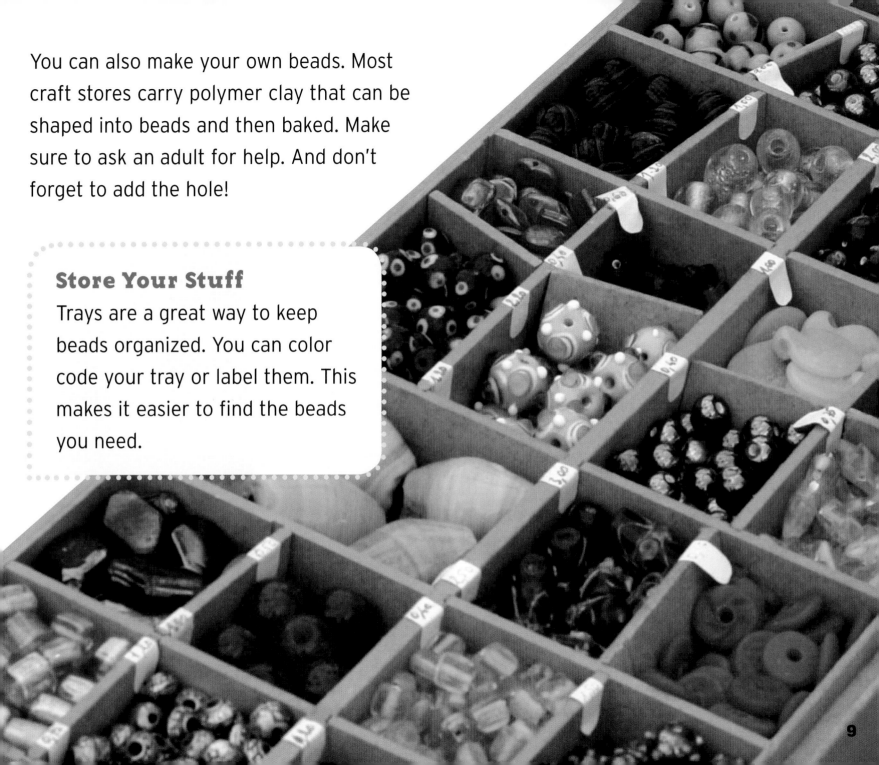

You can also make your own beads. Most craft stores carry polymer clay that can be shaped into beads and then baked. Make sure to ask an adult for help. And don't forget to add the hole!

Store Your Stuff

Trays are a great way to keep beads organized. You can color code your tray or label them. This makes it easier to find the beads you need.

The Long and Short of It

Once you have gathered your beads, you can begin stringing them. This is called threading. Thread is the material that holds your beads together. Almost anything that is long, thin, and flexible can be used as thread, even ribbon or shoelaces.

There are many types of threads to choose from. Nylon thread, often called nymo, is very strong and comes in many colors. It can look like fishing line or dental floss. Clear nylon thread can't be seen at all, unless you look carefully. Silk thread is soft and elegant and goes best with precious beads like pearls. Elastic cord is great for slip-on jewelry such as bracelets.

Colorful thread can add excitement to your beaded creations. Choose a thread that will complement the colors in the beads you are using.

The stringing material you choose must thread through the holes in your beads. Pick a thread that is thick if you are using large beads and thin if you are using small beads. Make sure that your thread will not fray or fall apart with use. If you need more help, ask a salesperson in your local craft or beading store to show you the thread they have available.

Getting to the Point

Threading beads can be difficult. Some beads have very tiny holes. Beading needles are helpful to guide your thread easily through the holes. You can thread many beads onto a needle at one time to make your work go faster. Beading needles are similar to sewing needles, because they have a sharp point at one end and an eye at the other. The eye of the needle holds your thread.

Beading needles can be found in a variety of lengths and thicknesses. When choosing a needle for your project, pick one with an eye big enough for the size of thread you will be working with. Make sure that the needle and eye will fit through your bead holes.

Needle Knows

Store your beading needles point down in a pin cushion. This will keep your needles from rolling away and you from getting poked!

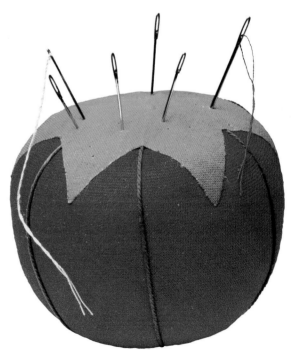

Specialized beading needles help you accomplish difficult tasks. Big-eye needles allow you to bead with even the thickest cord or thread because the entire needle is the eye.

You don't always have to use a beading needle. If you are using firm or thick thread and your bead holes are large, you can sometimes bead without a needle.

13

Additional Tools and Materials You'll Need

- A pair of scissors

- Beeswax to run along the length of your thread to prevent fraying and help beads glide smoothly onto the thread

- A glue gun to dab glue that will dry clear onto your finishing knots so that they will not unravel

- Small jewelry pliers to help you attach finishing clasps to your thread

- Beading awl, knotting tweezers, or a strong, long pin to help you create knots in your thread

Where To Get It

Beading supplies can be found at craft stores, art supply stores, jewelry supply stores, and beading stores. A lot of supplies are also available on the Internet.

- Small trays or containers to sort your beads for easy access

- Good lighting

- A rough piece of cloth to work on; this will prevent loose beads from rolling all over your work surface

Let's Begin Beading

Let's string some beads. Take out your beads and some thread. Nylon thread is good to begin with. Now create a place to arrange your beads, by laying a piece of cloth down on your work area. The cloth keeps your beads from rolling away as you work, so rough cloth like corduroy works best. Begin by placing different beads next to each other on the cloth. Be creative. Put some small beads next to a bigger bead. Feature a special bead in the center of your arrangement. Try different combinations of beads that look exciting to you. As you play with your bead arrangement, patterns of color, shape, and texture will begin to emerge. There are no rules!

When your bead arrangement sparkles with beauty, you are ready to thread your beads. The first bead you string will serve as the tension bead. This bead is removed at the end of the project so it should not be a bead from your design.

A tension bead, or stopper bead, acts as an anchor, preventing the beads from falling off your thread. Pass your thread through the hole of the tension bead, positioning the bead about 4-6 inches (10-15 centimeters) from the end of the thread. Loop the beginning of the thread through the tension bead again. Now string the rest of your beads. Simply slip the beginning of your thread through the hole of each bead, according to the arrangement you have chosen. Finally, knot the end of your thread.

Congratulations, you have made a strand of beads!

Eye of the Needle

Beading needles help you string your beads easily. You will not need to use a needle in every beading project. If you are using a needle, thread your needle by inserting one end of a length of thread through the eye of the needle. Then, pull several inches of thread through the eye so the thread will not slip out again.

Threading a needle is tricky, so don't be discouraged if you can't do it on the first try. Here are some tips to make threading a cinch:

- Work under good light so that you can see your needle eye and thread clearly.

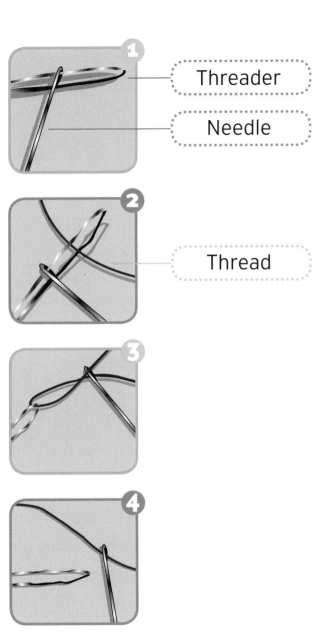

Threader

Needle

Thread

- Use a threader. A threader is a big loop that helps you thread your needle quickly and easily. First, insert the threader into the needle eye. Then, insert your thread into the big loop of the threader, and pull the threader loop back out of the needle eye. You have a threaded needle.

- Use beeswax on fine thread. Run beeswax along the length of your thread to keep it from fraying.

- If you still have trouble, ask an adult for help.

Lots of Knots

Some beading projects require knots. Knots are often used to attach special jewelry components called findings to your piece. They also work great as a simple type of closure when you are ready to wear your beads. Knots can be used to separate beads from one another and to hold them securely in place. In fine pearl necklaces, there are knots between each pearl. All these knots protect the pearls from rubbing together. The knots also prevent the pearls from sliding off if the thread were to break. It is up to you to decide how many knots to use and where they will go. You may choose to use lots of knots, only a few, or none at all.

If you are using knots, place them as close as you can to your beads so your beads don't slide around. Remember that knotting takes up thread. If your project requires many knots, add an inch or two of extra thread to the finished length to account for the knots.

Knot Close

Making your knots very close to your beads is important. Use a tool called a beading awl or knotting tweezers to help. A strong pin will do as well. When you are ready to make a knot, make a loose overhand knot and insert your pin, tweezers, or awl into the knot. Use your tool to slide the knot as close as you can to your bead while tightening the knot. Remove your tool from the knot and tighten the knot firmly.

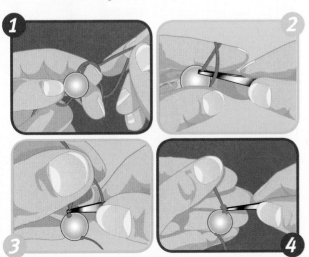

Here are some basic knots to get you started with your beading:

- **Overhand knot:** Cross one strand over and then under the other, bringing that end back through the loop that is formed.

- **Double knot:** Make an overhand knot twice with the same strand of thread.

- **Adjustable sliding knot:** Start with two strings. Tie one string to the other in an overhand knot. Repeat on the opposite side. Pull the strands tight enough so the knots do not unravel.

Findings, Clasps, and Closures

Do you have a bracelet with a clasp on it that allows you to take the bracelet on and off? The clasp is a finding. Findings are small metal parts that finish your beaded creation, keep it together, and make it unique. There are many different types of findings, each with a special purpose.

Clasps allow you to take jewelry on and off. They come in many different styles. Some clasps to look for are hook and eye, S clasps, lobster claw, toggle, and barrel clasps.

Jump rings and split rings are used to connect clasps to your jewelry and join different pieces of jewelry together.

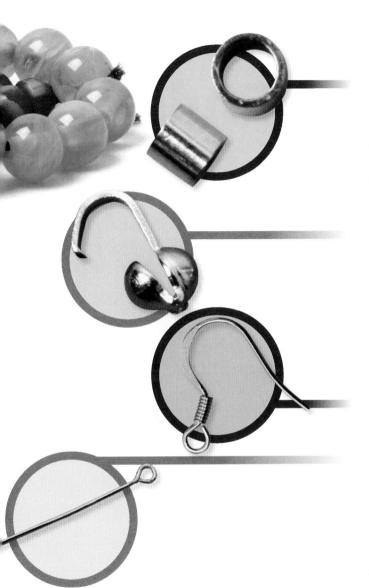

Crimps are a great way to start and end a strand of beads. Crimp beads make a smooth transition to your clasp. Crimps are secured by giving them a strong squeeze with pliers.

Bead tips, clam shells, and end caps are ending components that hide the knots at the end of your beaded strand. Bead tips, clam shells, and end caps also provide a way to connect other findings, like clasps, to your jewelry.

Earring findings are for beaded earring jewelry.

Eye pins and head pins are used to assemble earrings and beaded dangles.

Tying Up Loose Ends

Let's look at how to turn your simple strand of beads into jewelry. Perhaps you have threaded some large beads onto a chunky piece of ribbon. Simply tying the ribbon around your neck with a beautiful bow is an easy way to create a neckpiece. Close friends like to tie on their friendship bracelets with permanent knots and never take them off.

There are many other ways to create a closure. You can use clasps, which are the most common closures and come in a variety of finishes such as gold, silver, and copper. With so many to choose from, finding the right clasp can be as much fun as picking the beads.

- Try making your own closure with a unique button and a beaded loop of thread.

- Finish a leather bracelet with a pair of adjustable slide knots. (See project #2.)

- If you make a very long strand of beads that can easily go over your head, you do not need a closure.

How Do I Fix That?

Most beading mistakes are very easy to fix, so don't be afraid to experiment and take some chances. Follow these tips to keep your beading project on track:

- When cutting a length of thread, make sure that it is long enough to complete your project. Measure out the length that you want your finished piece to be, plus several extra inches for making knots and tying up loose ends.

- Work slowly and carefully so that your thread and beads don't get tangled.

- Do not try to force needles through bead holes that are not big enough.

- Ask an adult if you need help with gluing, cutting, or threading.

Beaded Pen and Pencil Wraps

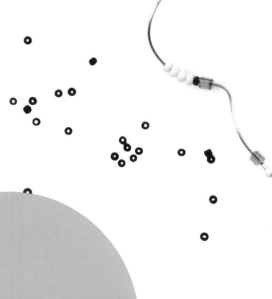

Materials

- Pen or pencil

- Colored wire

- Alphabet and regular beads

1. Cut a 4 inch (10 cm) piece of wire.

2. With a needle-nose pliers, bend down the tip of one end of the wire.

3. String your beads onto the wire to spell out a name or special word.

4. Once you have all your beads on the wire, clip off any extra wire, leaving just enough to bend over the last bead.

5. Now wrap the wire into a tight spiral around your pen or pencil.

Leather Bracelet

Materials

- 8-12 beads
- Leather cord (available at fabric and craft stores)
- Scissors

1. Wrap a piece of leather cord around your wrist 2 times and cut the cord to this length.

2. String your beads onto the leather cord. Slide the beads to the middle of the cord and tie an adjustable slide knot on either side of the group of beads.

3. Try on your bracelet. You can slide the knots to adjust the size of the bracelet if necessary.

4. Snip off any extra cord.

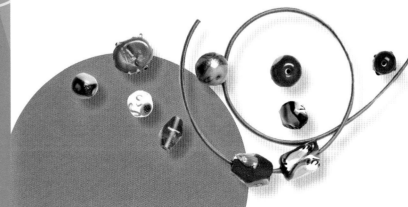

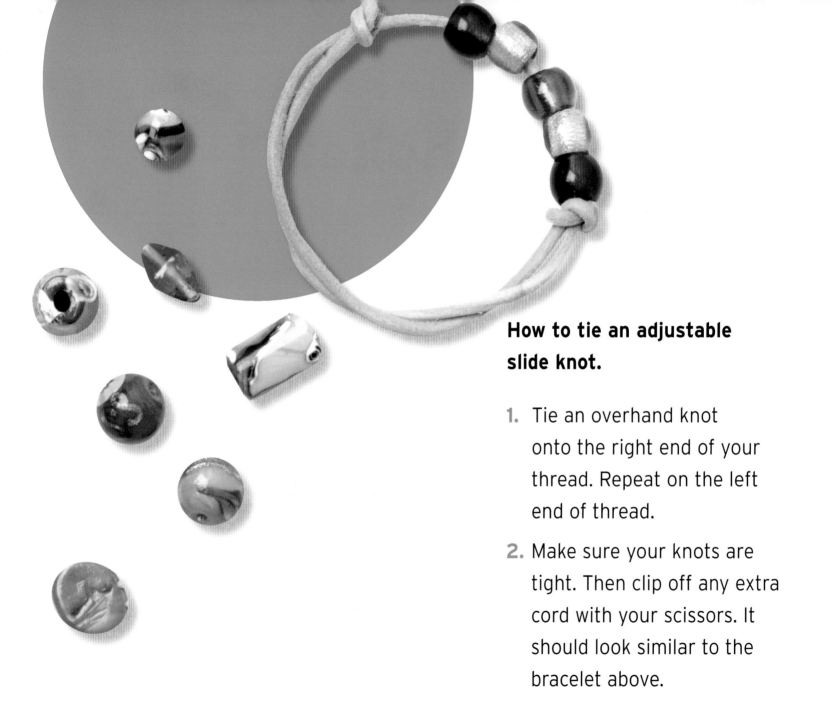

How to tie an adjustable slide knot.

1. Tie an overhand knot onto the right end of your thread. Repeat on the left end of thread.

2. Make sure your knots are tight. Then clip off any extra cord with your scissors. It should look similar to the bracelet above.

Simple Choker or Bracelet

Materials

- Nylon or similar thread

- Flexible needle

- Clasp

- Scissors

- Small beads (beads with too big a hole will not work well with nylon)

- Clear fingernail polish

1. Begin arranging your beads by laying them out on a towel so they won't roll around. When you are happy with your bead arrangement, cut a piece of nylon thread that is double the length you would like your necklace or bracelet to be, plus 20 inches (51 cm).

2. Thread your flexible needle and pull the thread through until it is doubled and the ends are even. Tie a double knot to the loop of one half of a clasp, leaving a tail 5 inches (13 cm) long.

3. Now you are ready to string your beads according to the arrangement you have designed.

4. When you are done stringing your beads make sure the necklace or bracelet is the length that you would like it to be.

5. When you are ready to end your necklace or bracelet, thread the needle through the loop of the other half of the clasp two times. Now pass the needle down through the last three beads. While holding onto the clasp, gently pull on the nylon to take up slack.

6. Tie a double knot around the thread in between the third and fourth beads.

7. Cut off the spare thread that holds the needle.

8. Thread the needle onto the 5-inch (13-cm) tail.

9. Now send the needle through the last three beads.

10. Make a double knot behind the third bead exactly like you did in step 6.

11. Put a little clear nail polish on the knots, let it dry completely, and trim the excess thread.

Beaded Safety Pins

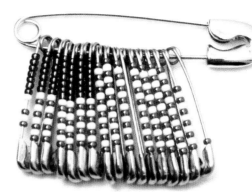

Materials

- Ten 1½ inch safety pins
- Two different colors of tiny beads
- Needle-nose pliers
- Flat-head screwdriver

1. Slide your beads onto the safety pins according to the star pattern. One color of bead will make the star, the other color will make the background.

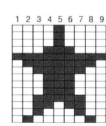

2. Each numbered column corresponds to a safety pin.

3. On your first pin, slide on four beads of color 1, one bead of color 2, and nine beads of color 1.

4. Your second pin will have four beads of color 1, two beads of color 2, seven beads of color 1, and one bead of color 2.

5. Once all the beads are in place, close the safety pin.

6. Use the needle-nose pliers to pinch the end of the safety pin so it will not pop open later.

7. When you are done beading all your pins, you are ready to group them onto the last remaining safety pin.

8. Use the flat-head screwdriver to slightly pry apart the coils at the end of this main pin.

9. Starting with pin number 1, slip the loop of the beaded safety pin onto the main pin.

10. Pull the beaded pin down to the loop at the base of the pin.

11. Now, pull it around the loop and up the back side. Repeat this for each beaded safety pin.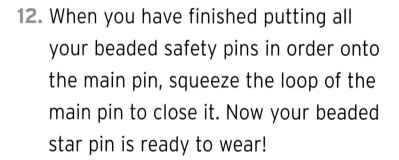

12. When you have finished putting all your beaded safety pins in order onto the main pin, squeeze the loop of the main pin to close it. Now your beaded star pin is ready to wear!

Global Beading

The Ndebele people of South Africa are the most prolific beadworkers in the world. They create entire pieces of clothing out of woven beads. The Ndebele also use their beadwork to decorate everyday objects such as dolls, utensils, and pottery. They have developed a distinctive style using bold geometric shapes in the colors of blue, black, red, and yellow.

In Thailand, flowers are used as beads. Flower-bead garlands known as pomelai are an important part of Thai culture. They decorate people, temples, and taxicabs. During the Thai New Year, pomelai are used to decorate beautiful parade floats. The small white Mali flower is strung on white cotton thread, using a very long needle, to create these garlands. Because the flowers quickly dry out, pomelai only last for a few days.

One type of bead can be found almost anywhere around the world—the eye bead. Eye beads are small round beads that look like a tiny eye. This type of bead is extremely old and has been a favorite among beadworkers for thousands of years. Many cultures believe that eye beads provide protection from evil spirits.

Traditional Laos New Year's costume

A Carnival of Beads

Every year, revelers descend on New Orleans, Louisiana, for weeks of parties and parades throughout the city. This holiday season is known as Carnival and ends with the biggest party of all, Mardi Gras. The main highlights of Mardi Gras are the parades. Atop elaborate papier-mâché floats, costumed riders toss thousands of beaded necklaces to the cheering crowds. Everywhere, people jostle to catch the beads as they fly through the air. Everyone wants to catch as many necklaces as they can and wear them all at once.

The inexpensive strands of colorful plastic beads are worn like fancy diamond necklaces during this holiday.

"Throw Me Something, Mister"

Catching beads at a Mardi Gras parade is not easy. Many people compete for the necklaces thrown from the floats. It helps to catch the attention of the float riders so they will toss some beads in your direction.

Everyone Loves Beads

Beads are not just used in jewelry. You can find beads on clothing, accessories, and even household items. Since beads are inexpensive and readily available, beaded fashion does not have to be costly to buy or make. However, some of the most expensive clothing on the planet is made with beads. Fancy dresses can have thousands of beads embroidered onto them by hand, taking many weeks to make. Keep your eye out for how beads are used in fashion where you shop.

Oscar Night

One of the biggest nights of the year for movies and fashion, the Academy Awards features some of entertainment's most famous celebrities. The stars want to look their best to walk down the red carpet and hopefully take home an Oscar. The night is a showcase for the latest and most beautiful in designer clothing. Look closely and you will find examples of exquisite beadwork decorating the gowns of many of the stars.

Bob Mackie's Beaded Wonders

Known as "the boss of beads," "the sultan of sequins," and "the rajah of rhinestones," Bob Mackie's dazzling gowns are the ultimate in glamour and magnificence. His unique style consists of covering an entire outfit in glittering beads. Mackie has created thousands of colorful costumes for TV, film, and the stage. Stars love his work. He has dressed many stars including Cher, Sharon Stone, Madonna, and even Barbie.

One of his favorite beads is the tiny bugle bead. Bugle beads are small, narrow beads used for intricate designs. He uses bugle beads often to create a beaded fringe around his gowns. His creations look as if they are dripping with beads. Most of his beaded gowns are made by at least four people and take up to four weeks to complete. Thousands of beads are used to make one dress.

What Happened When?

| 3700 B.C. | 1000 A.D. | 1300 | 1600 | 1750 | 1900 |

3700 The earliest known beads are made in what is now Kenya, Africa. They are made of ostrich shell.

1308 A European bead maker's guild is formed to protect the rights of bead workers.

1760 Native Americans trade using beads. A 6-foot (2-meter) strand of beads will buy one beaver pelt.

1644–1911 During the Qing dynasty in China, top officials wore Buddhist rosaries with large beads called Buddha heads.

900 In Mexico and Central America, a counting device called an abacus is made with corn kernel beads.

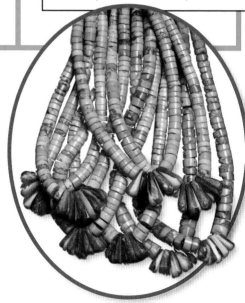

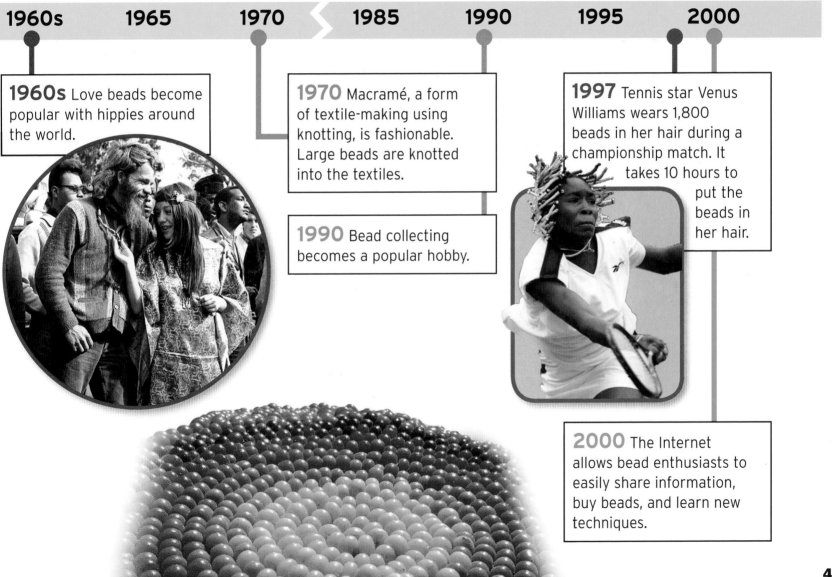

| 1960s | 1965 | 1970 | 1985 | 1990 | 1995 | 2000 |

1960s Love beads become popular with hippies around the world.

1970 Macramé, a form of textile-making using knotting, is fashionable. Large beads are knotted into the textiles.

1990 Bead collecting becomes a popular hobby.

1997 Tennis star Venus Williams wears 1,800 beads in her hair during a championship match. It takes 10 hours to put the beads in her hair.

2000 The Internet allows bead enthusiasts to easily share information, buy beads, and learn new techniques.

43

Fun Beading Facts

Moldavite beads are created from the green and black glass that forms when a meteorite hits the surface of Earth.

Sea beans are seeds that are found in the rainforest of Costa Rica. These seeds drift for months or years and travel for hundreds of miles over the world's oceans. They are collected and used as beads in jewelry.

Ghana

In Ghana, boys make special beads to give to girls they like. Girls wear a lot of beads to attract a boyfriend.

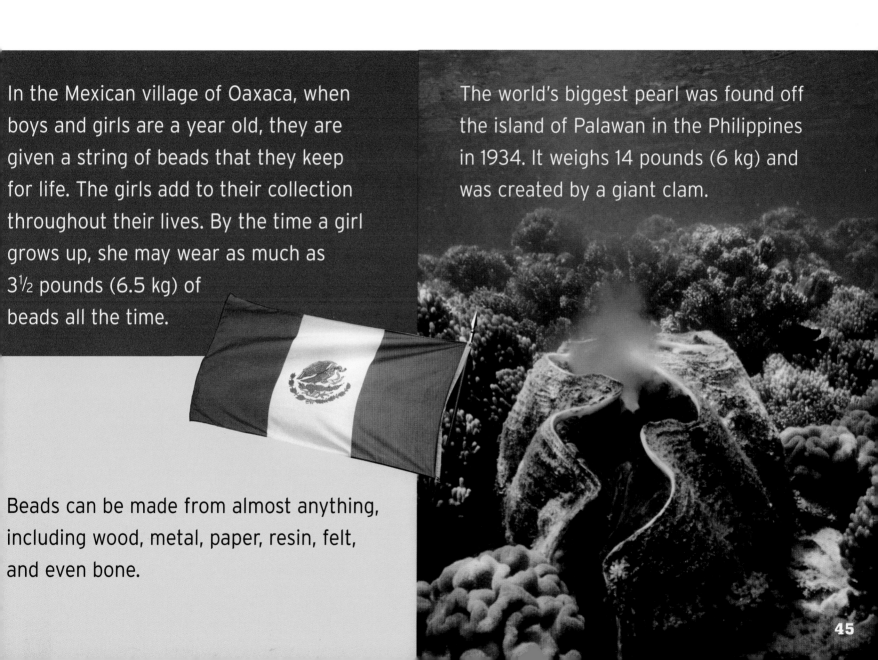

In the Mexican village of Oaxaca, when boys and girls are a year old, they are given a string of beads that they keep for life. The girls add to their collection throughout their lives. By the time a girl grows up, she may wear as much as 3½ pounds (6.5 kg) of beads all the time.

The world's biggest pearl was found off the island of Palawan in the Philippines in 1934. It weighs 14 pounds (6 kg) and was created by a giant clam.

Beads can be made from almost anything, including wood, metal, paper, resin, felt, and even bone.

Beading Words to Know

beading awl: a long, thin tool used to make knots

beading needle: a tool with a sharp point at one end and an eye at the other

big eye needle: a beading needle designed to be used with very thick thread

bugle beads: a small bead used for intricate beaded designs

closure: the way that a piece of jewelry is fastened together

earring findings: findings used as attachments to create earrings

earwires: the part of the earring that fits into the ear

end cap: a finding that hides the knots at the end of a beaded strand

eye pin: a finding shaped like a pin with a loop at the end; used to create dangles

findings: jewelry components used to finish beaded jewelry and hold it together

finishing knot: any knot that is used to end a piece of jewelry; usually a double knot

head pin: a finding shaped like a pin and used to create dangles

hemp cord: a thicker type of thread made from hemp fiber

jewelry pliers: a hand tool used to hold, bend, or cut wire

jump rings: small metal coiled rings used to attach jewelry parts together

knot: used to secure beads and findings, also used decoratively in macramé

knotting tweezers: used to make secure tight knots next to beads

leather cord: a thick thread made of leather

macramé: a form of textile making using knotting

moldavite: a type of glass bead created when a meteorite hits Earth

nymo: common nylon beading thread

overhand knot: a knot formed by making a loop and pulling the end through

silk thread: delicate beading thread made from silk

split rings: small metal rings used to attach jewelry parts together

tension bead: bead used to anchor the thread so that the strung beads do not fall off

thread: any string, cord, or wire that the beads are strung on

threader: a tool used to help thread a needle

threading: putting beads on a thread

tiger tail wire: nylon covered wire

Other Words to Know

abacus: a counting device made of beads on rods held in a frame

accessories: handbags, jewelry, shoes

catacombs: underground burial tombs

complement: something that completes, makes up a whole, or brings to perfection

exquisite: intricate, beautiful, as in a design

fray: to unravel

guild: a group of merchants or craftsmen, especially before 1500, that worked in the same trade

oblong: ellipse, elongated circle

prolific: of a great abundance

revelers: people at a party having fun

wampum: small beads strung together in designs to record events; sometimes used as money

Where To Learn More

AT THE LIBRARY

Davis, Jane. *The Complete Guide to Beading Techniques*. Iola, Wis.: Krause Publications, 2001.

Campbell, Jean. *Getting Started Stringing Beads*. Loveland, Colo.: Interweave Press, 2005.

ON THE ROAD

The Bead Museum
5754 W. Glenn Drive
Glendale, AZ 85301
623/931-2737

The Bead Museum Washington, D.C.
The Jenifer Building
400 Seventh St. N.W.
Washington, DC 20004

ON THE WEB

For more information on BEADING, use FactHound to track down Web sites related to this book.

1. Go to www.facthound.com
2. Type in this book ID: 0756516889
3. Click on the *Fetch It* button.

Your trusty FactHound will fetch the best Web sites for you!

INDEX

ABOUT THE AUTHOR
Benjamin Ashfield works as a graphic designer specializing in Web site design. His work is available online at partially.org. He lives in New York City with his partner Tammy who is a jewelry designer and his son Loren.